The 72 Names of God

A Treasury of Timeless Wisdom

for **Kids**

For further information:

The Kabbalah Centre
155 E. 48th St., New York, NY 10017
1062 S. Robertson Blvd., Los Angeles, CA 90035

1.800.Kabbalah www.kabbalah.com

First Edition
April 2006
Printed in Canada
ISBN1-57189-543-4

Design: HL Design (Hyun Min Lee) www.hldesignco.com

The 72 Names of God

of God

A Treasury of Timeless Wisdom

for
Kids

Technology for the Soul™

Yehuda Berg with **Dev Ross**

K
KABBALAH
PUBLISHING

DEDICATION

To David, Moshe, Chana, Yacov and Esther

ACKNOWLEDGMENTS

By Yehuda Berg

I would like to thank the many people who have made this book possible.

First and foremost, I am eternally grateful to Rav and Karen Berg, my parents and teachers. Your guidance and support nurture me and the many others who connect with your love and wisdom.

To Michael Berg, my brother, for your friendship, vision and strength. You are a deep well of inspiration and encouragement for me.

To my wife, Michal, for your love and commitment, power, beauty, and clarity. You are the heartbeat of our home and family.

David, Moshe, Channa, Yakov, and Esther, the precious gifts in my life, who remind me every day how much there is to be done to ensure that tomorrow will be better than today.

Billy Phillips, one of my closest friends, for your help in making this book possible. The contribution you make to The Kabbalah Centre every day and in so many ways is appreciated far more than you could possibly know.

To Hyun Lee and Esther Sibilia, whose contributions made the physical quality and integrity of everything we do live up to the spiritual heritage of this incredible wisdom that has been passed on to me by my father, Rav Berg.

I want to thank all the team at PGW for their vision and support. Your proactive efficiency gives us the confidence to produce more and more books on Kabbalah so that the world can benefit from this amazing wisdom.

To Paul Caplan-Bennet, a dedicated volunteer, who introduced me to Dev Ross, and to Dev, a wonderful children's writer—it is a gift to be able to bring the child's point of view to life. And to Phyllis Henrici for sharing her years of publishing experience with me.

My gratitude to those responsible for the artwork in this book: Gary Kopervas for the drawings; all the kids of SFK for creating such delightful paintings; and Ellen Sassa for her wise selection of the paintings we used.

To all the Chevre at The Kabbalah Centres worldwide—the evenings we share together in study fuel my passion to bring the power of Kabbalah to the world. You are a part of me and my family no matter where you might be.

To the students who study Kabbalah all over the world—your desire to learn, to improve your lives, and to share with the world is an inspiration. The miracles I hear from you every day make everything I do worthwhile.

ACKNOWLEDGMENTS

By Dev Ross

Being a part of this book's creation was both a joy and a journey, and most certainly a journey that could not have been made without the help of these wonderful individuals. I would like to thank Yehuda Berg for introducing me to the world of Kabbalah, Esther Sibilia for her passion for the Names and for being there every step of the way, Rachel Liberman for her organizational support, and my advocate, my advisor, and my dear friend, Paul Caplan-Bennett, whose personal relationship to Kabbalah is truly inspirational.

TABLE OF CONTENTS

TABLE OF CONTENTS

Page

tents

SPIRITUALITY FOR KIDS

The children who have painted these amazing works of art and who have been quoted in these pages have all been a part of Spirituality for Kids program. Spirituality for Kids, also known as SFK, is a free outreach program for kids ages 6 to 14 that is offered after school and on weekends. This unique program helps give young people the tools needed to make positive life choices. In weekly classes led by trained instructors, children learn how to become self-reliant and well adjusted. They learn to overcome problems and obstacles in their lives while setting the stage for their own happy and productive futures.

SFK is not just for children. Families who attend the program together become motivated to make both real and fundamental improvements in their lives.

Based on an ancient wisdom that explains the nature of universal spiritual laws, SFK uses the arts, science, music, history, and even pop culture to illustrate that peace and fulfillment are the birthright of all humanity.

www.sfk.org

PREFACE

Believing is seeing.

Doing is achieving.

If we believe in the Light within us, we will see, we will do, and we *will* achieve!

"Those who bring sunshine into the lives of others cannot keep it from themselves."
—James M. Barrie, author of *Peter Pan* (1860-1937)

RATTLING THE GATES OF HEAVEN

There once was a young boy named David who was very sick. His parents took him to doctor after doctor but not one of them could help David get well.

Now, it so happened that a wise old man lived in the same town as David. The old man wasn't a doctor but people from all around came to him for his wondrous cures. In fact, many people believed the old man could talk to angels!

So David's father took him to see the old man.

The kind old man looked deep into David's eyes. He could see that David was very sick, maybe too sick to help, but still he would try.

That night the old man prayed for David so hard that his spirit shot straight up to the gates of heaven. But the gates were not open. In fact, there was a big lock on them.

The old man rattled the gates and called out to the angels to come and open them, but not a single angel came. He tried to break the lock but it was too strong. And then the old man realized that the locked gates could mean only one thing: They were closed to his prayers for David.

The next morning when he heard the news, David's father began to cry. "There has to be a way," he said. "There has to be a way to break into heaven to save my David! Please! Please! You must try again!"

The old man promised he would try again. But what could he do differently? How could he, an honest man, break into heaven? And then he got an idea.

The old man went to the worst part of town where thieves roamed the streets. Instead of stealing his money, the thieves listened to what the old man had to say.

Before long, ten of the thieves followed the old man back to his house. Even though they wanted to, they did not rob the old man's house. Instead, they sat with him and prayed for David.

The next morning, after the thieves had left the old man's house, David's father raced up.

"It's David!" he cried. "My David is well again!" David's father thanked the old man again and again before running off to tell the rest of the town about his son's miraculous recovery.

. . . .

Though the story is over, some of us might be wondering how the prayers of thieves could help David.

The answer is this: The thieves' prayers were able to break the lock on the gate so that the old man's prayers could sneak into heaven!

How are the thieves in the story like us? They're like us in that they represent our selfish parts.

Just like the thieves, our selfish parts are the key to unlocking heaven's gate. If we work hard to change from being selfish to being caring and sharing, the key in the lock turns, the gates of heaven swing open, and endless blessings and miracles pour down around us.

The things about us that are unhelpful and hurtful are our key to changing ourselves for the better.

TO SHARE OR NOT TO SHARE: THAT IS THE QUESTION!

Chris finally got the Xbox he'd been wanting for like forever but now his little brother Max was begging him to let him play, too. Chris knew it was nice to share but a loud voice inside of him, the voice of the Opponent, made him say . . .

"No way, Max! You can NOT play with my Xbox! It's mine, all mine!"

Max didn't understand why his big brother was being so selfish. Max wouldn't do anything bad to the Xbox. In fact, he was a pretty good player.

Chris could see he'd really hurt Max's feelings. Then he heard another voice inside of him. It was softer than the voice of the Opponent and it told him that if he shared his Xbox with his little brother, it would make them both happy.

So, instead of listening to the voice of the Opponent, Chris listened to the voice of the Good Guy inside of him. Sharing did make him happy and it moved him closer to the Light.

The Light? What Light?

The Light is the cause of all good things. It's an energy source that causes happiness and love. It's also the cause of good health and good relationships with parents, teachers, and friends.

When we change the things about us that are unhelpful and hurtful, we connect to the Light's endless blessings.

Okay, so we want to change. How do we do it?

We do it with the tools called THE 72 NAMES OF GOD.

The 72 Names of God help us change into helpful, sharing people so we can connect to the Light.

In the boxes on the next page we will see a series of shapes that may look strange to us. These shapes are Aramaic letters. When put in the right order, these letters make up the 72 Names of God. The 72 Names of God are not names like Joshua or Sarah or Amber or Ralph. They are spiritual, mystical names that help us quiet the Opponent's voice so we can listen to our Good Guy voice.

Now some of you may be asking, "Why do we want to listen to our Good Guy voice again?"

Because when we listen to our Good Guy voice it moves us closer to the Light, to happiness, to all things good!

Okay, back to the 72 Names.

We don't have to understand the letters to use them. All we have to do is follow the directions.

Here we go!

We take the first letter from the first box (which is ו), and the first letter from the second box (which is ה), and the first letter from the third
box (which is ו). We put them together and we have the first secret
Holy Name of God.

Let's go for the second Name. We take the second letter from the first
box (which is י), the second letter from the second box (which is כ),
and the second letter from the third box (which is י). We put them
together and we have the second Holy Name of God.

These directions explain how we unlock a very powerful secret knowledge. This secret knowledge will help us make our lives the best they
can be!

וַיִּסַּע מַלְאַךְ הָאֱלֹהִים הַהֹלֵךְ לִפְנֵי מַחֲנֵה יִשְׂרָאֵל וַיֵּלֶךְ מֵאַחֲרֵיהֶם
וַיִּסַּע עַמּוּד הֶעָנָן מִפְּנֵיהֶם וַיַּעֲמֹד מֵאַחֲרֵיהֶם:

God's angel had been traveling in front of the Israelite camp,
but now it moved and went behind them. The pillar of cloud
thus moved from in front of them and stood at their rear.

מ	מ	ע	א	שׁ	ל	א	ו	1
ד	פּ	ע	ח	ר	פּ	ל	י	2
מ	ג	מ	ר	א	ג	ה	ס	3
א	י	ו	י	ל	י	י	ע	4
ח	ה	ד	ה	ו	מ	ם	מ	5
ר	ם	ה	ם	י	ח	ה	ל	6
י	ו	ע	ו	ל	ג	ה	א	7
ה	י	ג	י	ר	ה	ל	ר	8
ם	ע	ן	ס	מ	י	ר	ה	9

וַיָּבֹא בֵּין מַחֲנֵה מִצְרַיִם וּבֵין מַחֲנֵה יִשְׂרָאֵל וַיְהִי הֶעָנָן וְהַחֹשֶׁךְ וַיָּאֶר
אֶת הַלָּיְלָה וְלֹא קָרַב זֶה אֶל זֶה כָּל הַלָּיְלָה:

It came between the Egyptian and the Israelite camps. There was
cloud and darkness that night, blocking out all visibility. All that
night [the Egyptians and Israelites] could not approach one another.

ה	כ	ל	ה	ל	י	ל	ה
ק	ר	ב	ז	ה	א	ל	ז
ה	ל	י	ל	ה	ו	ל	א
שׁ	ר	ו	י	א	ר	א	ת
י	ה	ע	ג	ן	ו	ה	ח
י	שׁ	ר	א	ל	ו	י	ה
ו	ב	י	ן	מ	ח	נ	ה
ח	ג	ה	מ	צ	ר	י	ם
ו	י	ב	א	ב	י	ן	מ
1	**2**	**3**	**4**	**5**	**6**	**7**	**8**

וַיֵּט מֹשֶׁה אֶת יָדוֹ עַל הַיָּם וַיּוֹלֶךְ יְהוָה אֶת הַיָּם בְּרוּחַ קָדִים עַזָּה כָּל הַלַּיְלָה וַיָּשֶׂם אֶת הַיָּם לֶחָרָבָה וַיִּבָּקְעוּ הַמָּיִם:

Moses extended his hand over the sea. During the entire night, God drove back the sea with a powerful east wind, transforming the sea bed into dry land. The waters were divided.

3

י	ה	י	י	ה	ו	ד	ו	1
ב	י	ל	ם	י	ל	ו	י	2
ק	ם	ה	ע	ם	ר	ע	ט	3
ע	ל	ו	ז	ב	י	ל	מ	4
ו	וו	י	ה	ר	ה	ה	שׁ	5
ה	ר	שׁ	כ	ו	ו	י	ה	6
מ	ב	ם	ל	וו	ה	ם	א	7
י	ה	א	ה	ק	א	ו	ת	8
ם	ו	ת	ל	ד	ת	י	י	9

INSTRUCTIONS FOR USING THE 72 NAMES OF GOD

1. We sit in a chair.

2. We think about what's bothering us or what we'd like to change in our lives.

3. We find the Name in the book that will help us with our problem.

4. We let our minds become quiet and still. We concentrate on our breathing.

5. We let our eyes rest on the Name we've chosen. We look at the letters from right to left.

6. We imagine the power of the Name filling us up inside.

7. We close our eyes and see the Name in our minds.

8. We open our eyes and look at the Name on the page once again.

9. We close our eyes again and see the Name in our minds once more. Now the Name is no longer on the page. Where is it?

10. We open our eyes. The Name is now inside of us. It will work with us to find the Light that is also inside of us.

And now, ladies and gentlemen, boys and girls, aunts, uncles, cousins, kin, countrymen—and, of course, anyone else reading this book—we give you **THE NAMES!**

THREE,

TWO,

ONE . . .

Blast

וידו

TIME
TRAVEL

1. TIME TRAVEL

"Making it better. Making up for it."
—Darren Valenzuela, age 9

When we use this Name, we'd best fasten our seat belt!

TEN . . . NINE . . . EIGHT . . . SEVEN . . . SIX . . . FIVE . . . FOUR . . . THREE . . . TWO . . . ONE . . . BLAST OFF!

We're blasting back in time! Now we grab a shovel and dig up all the bad stuff we've ever done. Once the bad stuff is all dug up, the Light can touch it and transform it into—*poof!*—a bright new future!

We use this Name to bring on a future full of joy!

CAPTURING THE
SPARKS

2. CAPTURING THE SPARKS

What do we want most out of life?

HAPPINESS?
LOVE?
FREEDOM?
ALL OF THE ABOVE?

But sometimes we feel like a giant vacuum cleaner is sucking out our life. We feel tired all the time. We feel bored. We don't feel like doing anything.

ENTER THIS NAME!

When we use this Name we pull into the gas station of Light and fill up! We are filled with divine energy. Now we are not tired! Now we are not bored! Now we're ready for ALL OF THE ABOVE!

MIRACLE
MAKING

3. MIRACLE MAKING

"Things that are impossible happen."
—*Malik, age 8*

Long ago, the Philistines and the Israelites were at war. The Philistines had a secret weapon . . . Goliath! Goliath was *nine* feet tall and covered with heavy armor. Every day, Goliath challenged the Israelites. If one of them could beat him, the Philistines would surrender. But even the strongest of the Israelites could not defeat such a giant. What were the Israelites to do?

A young shepherd boy named David came to the battle to bring food to his Israelite brothers. When he heard Goliath's challenge, he alone stepped forward to fight the giant.

David had no armor but he did have five stones and his slingshot. Goliath laughed at the sight of David, then ran toward him with his sword flashing.

Quickly, David put a stone in his slingshot and shot it toward the giant. The stone hit Goliath in his forehead and the mighty giant fell to the ground.

How did such a young boy think he could even face a giant? He did it by using the Names! But before he faced the giant, David had to face himself. He had to change himself *inside* in order to make great things happen *outside*.

> **We use this Name to make our own miracles!**

עולם

GETTING RID OF
NEGATIVE
THOUGHTS

4. GETTING RID OF NEGATIVE THOUGHTS

"I'm no good!"

"I want to hit my little brother!"

"I hate my mom!"

Like a tune we can't stop thinking about, harmful thoughts can run through our minds over and over again.

"I'm no good!"

"I want to hit my little brother!"

"I hate my mom!"

Just as we switch channels on a radio and change the tune, we can change the thoughts in our minds.

"I'm a good person."

"I want my little brother to be safe."

"I love my mom."

> We use this Name to turn off the bad tune! Now a song of Light rattles our bones and fills our whole body with joy!

HEALING

36

5. HEALING

"Healing could be physical or not physical."
—Celene, age 13

"To heal something with love, light, power."
—Lidir, age 6

I think good things about you, and you begin to heal.

You heal and my heart mends.

And . . . we are both better for it.

> We use the power of this Name to help heal ourselves and others.

DREAM
STATE

6. DREAM STATE

When we think about this Name and then go to sleep, our dreams will tell us all sorts of things.

They will tell us about our lives.

They will help us make choices.

They will help us become wise.

When we wake up in the morning, we will feel the brand-new batteries inside of us.

We'll feel recharged!

We'll feel excited about life!

We use this Name to tell our own future!

CONNECTING TO OUR SOUL

Amanda's life was a mess. She was in fifth grade and her parents were getting a divorce. Her dad was moving to a whole new city far away. Soon she would be expected to live in two different houses, in two different bedrooms, and have two sets of friends. If that wasn't bad enough, her grades were slipping. Instead of her usual A in math, she was getting a C minus! Everyone wanted to help her. Her teachers, her school counselor . . . But no matter how much she talked with them, her problem still remained. Her parents were splitting up and she was powerless to stop it. Her head was spinning! Her life was becoming meaningless.

Amanda needed order back in her life. She needed calm. So she thought about this Name. Night after night, she studied it until the Name burned in her like a dancing flame.

And then things got better. Her parents still got a divorce but Amanda was calm. Amanda was strong. She knew her parents loved her. She knew that no matter which parent she was with, all would be well. The Light was alive inside of her and she would be just fine.

We use this Name to create order out of confusion.

SENDING AWAY
NEGATIVE
ENERGY

8. SENDING AWAY NEGATIVE ENERGY

Most of us have heard the saying: Sticks and stones may break my bones but words will never hurt me.

But negative words and thoughts from others can hurt us. They can make us feel bad.

A Golden Circle of Protection surrounds our bodies. We can't see it, feel it, or touch it, but it's there just like the air we breathe.

When we concentrate on this Name, our Golden Circle protects us from dark forces, anger, and hatred. Bad words and thoughts bounce off us like rubber because we are protected by a circle of love!

We use this Name and are protected!

ANGELIC
POWERS

9. ANGELIC POWERS

*"When you're hurt or sick angels help you. They help poor people.
They give you miracles."*
—*Yesenia, age 13*

When we speak, act harshly
Are selfish and cruel
Dark angels surround us
Quick! Quick! Grab the tools!
This Name to guide us
Bright angels arrive
Loving words, loving acts
Makes the Light come alive!

We use this Name to find our positive angels!

אב״ד

PROTECTION
FROM THE
EVIL EYE

10. PROTECTION FROM THE EVIL EYE

Adam was really good at baseball. He was also popular with the girls.

Danielle was an excellent gymnast and her teachers really liked how well she participated in class.

Both Adam and Danielle knew that some kids in their schools were jealous of them.

Some girls were secretly hoping that Danielle would lose her next gymnastic competition.

Some boys were secretly hoping that Adam would drop the ball.

So Adam and Danielle used this special Name to keep the "evil eye" of envy and hatred away from them.

They also used the Name to keep themselves from casting their own evil eye toward anyone else.

Sending our own hurtful thoughts out toward others weakens our Golden Circle of Protection. It opens up holes in our protective armor and lets the bad thoughts of others in.

We use this Name for protection!

THROWING AWAY

EVIL'S LEFTOVERS

11. THROWING AWAY EVIL'S LEFTOVERS

Jesse and his twin brother, Justin, hardly ever fought. But somehow, now, while moving into their new bedroom in their new house, they were at each other's throats in the worst way. They were calling each other some pretty harsh names. Justin even got so mad that he hurled one of his soccer shoes right at Jesse's head. Though Jesse ducked the flying cleat, tears of hurt quickly collected in his eyes and Justin knew instantly that he had gone too far. He felt bad but he also felt something else, something strange. He looked down at his arm. The tiny blond hairs on it were standing on end and it felt like ants were crawling up and down his back. He had never felt anything like this before, and they had never fought like this before. What was going on?

That evening, the twins learned about the unhappy family who had once lived in their new house. The house had seen a lot of fighting. Their dad and mom even showed them a place in the wall that was still dented from a shoe being thrown.

That night, before they turned off the lights in their new bedroom, Jesse and Justin sat together and concentrated on this Name. They knew that the Name would help them cast off the anger that still lingered in their room.

It did, and they slept peacefully.

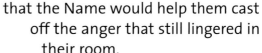

We use this Name and banish the "leftover bad stuff" from where we live.

UNCONDITIONAL
LOVE

12. UNCONDITIONAL LOVE

"You can't control it. Now matter how worse things get, you still care about them."
—Marcos, age 11

A young student, who thought himself very clever, once approached a very wise teacher and asked, "Can you teach me everything that is in the holy books, all the goodness, all the spirituality, everything, while I balance on one leg?" The wise teacher smiled and said, oddly enough, that he could. The young student didn't believe him for one second. He even let out a snort of laughter. Hah! But still, he balanced on one leg and with a mocking look on his face, told the wise teacher to begin. The wise teacher said simply, "Love thy neighbor as thyself. All the rest is commentary. Now go and learn." The young student's mouth fell open. In his heart he knew that what the wise teacher had said was absolute truth. The student swore that he'd follow the wise teacher's advice, and then ran off far wiser than he'd been only moments ago.

Love has the power to erase darkness. Love has the power to change our enemies. Love has the power to change us!

> **We use this Name to bring love into our lives and into the world.**

HEAVEN
ON EARTH

13. HEAVEN ON EARTH

"Talking about God, peace, love."
—Celene, age 13

"Watching television of Light."
—Ernesto Argota, age 12

Before peace can cover the planet, each and every one of us must find peace inside ourselves. Once we do, the peace inside of us will grow so large that it will have to spread to the next person and then to the next until, finally, the whole world is bathed in the Light of peace and love.

We can make our heaven on earth starting now, starting with me and you!

We use this Name to make earth heaven!

מ.ב.ה

STOP THE
FIGHTING

14. STOP THE FIGHTING

The commanding general lifted his sword and cried, "Charge! Take no prisoners! Kill the enemy! Destroy them! No mercy!" His brow knitted in determination, he lowered his sword and gazed out at the hordes of soldiers on the battlefield below. He expected to see a flood of bodies charging up the hill with brandished weapons. He expected flowing blood, shrieking cries.

Instead, he saw this:

All of the soldiers, every last one of them, had dropped their swords at their sides. Not a single one would attack. Not a single one would harm another living soul. During the night, this Name had passed between them like a warm breeze. By morning, the Name had become a whirlwind. The soldiers now knew that violence would never bring peace. Violence never brings anything but darkness. Only peace brings peace.

With no one to fight his battle, the general had to go home. But before he did, one soldier whispered the Name to him. The general was baffled by the Name but it stuck in his mind until it began to make its way to his heart.

We use this Name to help bring peace to the world.

15. LONG-RANGE VISION—EYES THAT CAN SEE FOR A MILE!

Should I or shouldn't I?

Is he the right friend for me?

Is she?

How do I know if I'm making the right decision?

I'm so confused!

In the long term doing this could be bad for me, but in the short term it sure sounds fun!

Doing this will make me popular right now! Who cares what happens after that?

Any of these sound familiar?

Using this Name helps us see things more clearly and make better choices for ourselves. And what's wrong with making the choices that make our lives better? Nothing!

> **We use this Name for the power of clear vision!**

GIVING
THE BOOT TO
SADNESS

16. GIVING THE BOOT TO SADNESS

Sometimes we just feel sad. Sometimes we don't want to do anything but sit around and feel guilty and shameful about ourselves.

But dusting ourselves off, climbing to our feet, and giving life a try again creates a giant Light inside of us. The Light gives the boot to sadness! Good energy fills us up!

We use this Name for the strength to stand up and try, and try again!

לא"ו

GREAT
ESCAPE

17. GREAT ESCAPE

"Me first! Me first!"

How many times have we heard that? Or . . .

"What do you think of ME?"

"What does this have to do with ME?"

"No one's more important than ME!"

Thinking ONLY of ourselves, having to have things OUR way, and believing that everything is about US puts us in prison! Yes, the me-me-me attitude puts us behind bars!

We can bust out of jail! We can throw off the chains!

We use this Name to find freedom!

Friendship!

Family!

Joy!

FERTILITY

18. FERTILITY

This kid had an idea that made him scream
From the tallest mountain,
"I have a dream!"

So he used this Name
(Of course he worked hard, too!)

And to his fulfillment it came!

His brilliant vision created . . .

_____

(What's YOUR dream or idea? YOU fill in the blank!)

Just as we use fertilizer and compost to enrich the soil to help plants grow, we use this Name to enrich our thoughts to help us grow in mind and spirit.

We use this Name if we really want our new ideas to work.

If we want help in creating a story assignment for school.

If we want an imaginative answer to a troubling problem.

> **We use this Name to improve the fertile soil of our minds so we can better reach our dreams and goals!**

DIALING GOD

לוי

19. DIALING GOD

"Have faith! Feel better!"
—Julius Valenzuela, age 11

If we call our friend and get a busy signal, we can figure it's because of one of three things:
1. He's on the Internet.
2. He doesn't have call waiting.
3. His phone is accidentally off the hook.

If we call God and get a busy signal, we can figure it's because of one of three things, too:
1. We've been using unkind words.
2. We've been using unkind behavior.
3. We've been stuck in the deeds of "me, me, me!"

Do we want a direct line to God with no busy signals? How about our prayers answered at the speed of Light?

We unplug our unkind words, our unkind behavior, and our deeds of ME and plug into the Light Line to God by using this Name! It's direct! And, best of all, it's free!

We use this Name for a direct line to God!

WINNING
BIG OVER
BAD HABITS

20. WINNING BIG OVER BAD HABITS

Would we rather overeat than exercise? Gobble down candy instead of veggies? Drink sugary soda instead of pure water? How come we know that overeating and candy and soda are BAD for us but we can't stop?

How about . . .

Cheating on tests? Smoking? Alcohol? Are they a problem?

This Name will help us win over all the bad habits we're fighting to get out of our lives.

> **We can do it if we use this Name!**

NO MORE
SICKNESS

21. NO MORE SICKNESS

No more smoking and smoking-related illness and death!

No more AIDS!

No more cancer!

No more pollution!

No more bombs!

No more hate and sadness and bad things that hurt people, animals, and our planet!

No more!

We use this Name to erase it all!

STOPPING THE **WRONG** PEOPLE FROM COMING INTO OUR LIVES

22. STOPPING THE WRONG PEOPLE FROM COMING INTO OUR LIVES

Tiffany thought Amber was the best friend she'd ever had. Amber walked with her to and from school, traded lunches with her when her mom insisted on putting soy cheese in her sandwiches, and even called James on the phone and asked him if he liked her or not. Yes, Amber was her best friend ever. Until recently, that is. Recently, Amber was being pretty bossy. She said that Tiffany should do her homework for her, and even help her cheat on a test because *she* had done so many nice things for her.

"Don't you think you owe me?" Amber asked with the cute baby voice she used whenever she wanted something. Tiffany didn't answer. She didn't know if she owed Amber anything or not. Did she?

Tiffany was going to tell Amber that maybe they shouldn't be friends anymore. She was going to do it any day now. She just needed to get brave enough.

If not-so-good people are coming into our lives, people who are stealing our energy or wanting us do things we don't want to do . . .

We use this Name to send them away with love and Light.

SHARING
THE FLAME

23. SHARING THE FLAME

Darkness and evil have no power when they're in the presence of the Light.

Have any of us ever awoken in our bedrooms at night and been scared? Maybe we're scared of the dark or, even worse, of the imaginary monsters that lurk under our beds or in our closets! But we bravely sit up and reach for our bedside light. We turn it on and—*poof!*—no more monsters.

If we share the wisdom of the Names with our friends and family, and then they share it with others, too, the Light spreads and spreads and spreads until . . .

POOF! No more monsters!

We use this Name to help share the Light with the whole world.

24. JEALOUSY

"Rage! It makes me feel mad. Unworthy."
—Mailk, age 8

I hate her because she has such pretty hair!

I hate him because he's so popular!

I want her life! She's famous!

I want his life! He's rich!

I want what they have and I hate them because they have it and I don't!

It's not fair!

We're all tied together. If we hate and if we're jealous, it hurts those around us, it hurts the world and mostly it hurts us.

> **We use this Name to help end suffering in the world.**

SPEAKING
OUR MINDS

25. SPEAKING OUR MINDS

"Say the truth!"
—Enriave Chavaurrig, age 13

"Saying to the people you love the truth and trust them."
—April, age 13

Twelve-year-old Jimmy was stealing beer from the refrigerator his parents kept in the garage. He told his best friend, Jorge, that it was all right because his parents drank so much they wouldn't notice if a beer or two went missing every now and then. Jimmy wanted Jorge to drink the beer with him but Jorge didn't want to. He told Jimmy that drinking beer wasn't good for them. After all, they were only twelve years old! But Jimmy kept stealing beer and drinking it. In fact, he was doing it more and more often. Jorge knew that what Jimmy was doing was wrong. He wanted to tell his friend in the worst way to stop or else he was going to have to tell someone, but every time he opened his mouth to speak, the words got stuck. Why wouldn't the words come out?

Do any of us need to tell someone the truth?

Do any of us need to hear the truth about ourselves?

We use this Name and the truth will set us free!

HOW TO
STRAIGHTEN UP
A BIG MESS

26. HOW TO STRAIGHTEN UP A BIG MESS

Are any of us tripping over our own feet?

Dropping our toast so the buttered side hits the floor?

Do we feel like we're riding a bike across a wobbly circus tightrope and are about to fall? And, even worse, there's no safety net?

If we answer "yes" to any of the above then it's important to know that . . .

There are ten dimensions or ten different realities. Three of them are outside of our physical world but *seven* are with us right here and now.

Seven, huh?

There are seven notes in a musical scale, seven primary colors, seven seas, seven major continents, and seven days in the week. Seven is a very important number!

When these seven dimensions get out of whack, we're out of balance and things can go wrong in our lives.

Let's be like Luke Skywalker in *Star Wars* and become "one with the Force"!

We use this Name to get back into balance and harmony with the world.

May the Force be with us!

SILENT
PARTNER

27. SILENT PARTNER

Silas came from a poor family. Though he was only eight years old, his father sent him off to tend the sheep that grazed a few miles from their hut. Bored with his lonely existence, Silas spent his time daydreaming of riches.

One evening as he walked home, daydreaming as usual, the warm air began to chill. Serpentine shadows wound through the trees then crept toward him with spindly fingers. Silas wanted to run, to cry out to his father, but his legs were leaden and his voice was frozen. Though he was silenced, the shadows were not. They promised him things. They promised him the riches he had always wanted—but at a price: his soul!

Silas wondered what good his soul was to him if tending sheep was all he ever did. Why not give up his soul for the riches that had, until now, only existed in his dreams?

He was about to allow the darkness in when something golden shimmered out of the darkness.

It burned white and hot until Silas could see this Name hovering among the trees! And what warmth it gave! The warmth from the Name was far more wondrous than anything offered by the darkness!

Silas embraced the Name and it filled him. Together, they pushed back the darkness until Silas was safely home.

All of us must be wise in choosing a "silent partner" to walk with us through life. This silent partner can be the Dark Force or the Light of the Creator, and they offer us different things:

The Dark Force may offer us riches, but if we're greedy and don't share, it will take away our spiritual Light.

The Light of the Creator will offer us spiritual wealth and even help us gain material riches. If we share our good fortune with others in the form of giving, endless blessings will be ours.

We share by giving charity, which is giving some of what we have to others less fortunate.

We use this Name to make the Light our silent partner.

28. SOUL MATE

"Having a special feeling."
—*April, age 13*

Grace lived in America.

Jaemyoung lived in South Korea.

They had lived completely different lives in completely different countries. When they accidentally bumped into one another on a crowded bus, they knew they would spend their lives together. And now they've been married forty years.

They were soul mates. Two halves that, when placed together, became one.

The energy of this Name will help you attract the other half of your soul.

We use this Name to help find true love, true friendship, and true partnership.

GETTING
RID OF
HATE

29. GETTING RID OF HATE

Carrying hate inside of us is like carrying a big load of wet laundry. It's cold, it's damp, and it's not very comfortable.

Hate eats us up inside. We can't think clearly because the red glare of hatred blinds our eyes.

Natural disasters such as floods, earthquakes, and even disease are caused by all the hate that has collected inside of people.

Our hate is not good for the world!

We use this Name to help get rid of hate!

אוּם

30. BUILDING BRIDGES

"Making up with someone by apologizing."
—*Jose Sabado*

Where Dylan lived, there were lots of bridges. There was a bridge to cross over the freeway to get to his school and another to get to his grandmother's house. There was a bridge over a storm channel on the way to his friend's house, and a bridge over a ravine on the way to his after-school job. And now the bridge builders were building a new bridge that would cross all the way over the water to land on the other side!

It was while watching this new bridge being built that Dylan thought, *I wonder if I could build a bridge all the way to God?*

So Dylan used this Name to build his bridge to God. He also used it to fix the broken bridges in his life. They were the ones that once led to people he was now in conflict with.

And Dylan discovered this: When he fixed the broken bridges, his bridge to God became stronger!

We use this Name to build our bridges to the Light!

FINISHING
WHAT WE
START

31. FINISHING WHAT WE START

"Genius is 1 percent inspiration and 99 percent perspiration."
—Thomas Alva Edison, inventor of the light bulb (1847-1931)

"I have tried a million schemes that will not work. I know everything that is no good. I work by elimination."
—Thomas Alva Edison

With only three months of formal education, Thomas Edison became one of the greatest inventors in history. Lucky for us, he was a man who never quit. He finished what he started even if it meant a million failures along the way.

We all have the power to finish what we start.

We use this Name to help us along the way!

 וישׂר

MEMORIES

32. MEMORIES

"Exile things in your past."
—Yesinia, age 13

This Name helps us erase the bad memories from our past. It also helps us remember the good things much better.

> We use this Name to help us learn our lesson so that we don't repeat the same mistake over and over again!

REVEALING
THE DARK SIDE

33. REVEALING THE DARK SIDE

Muriel could not tolerate dirt. Every day, she swept and dusted and polished her little house until it sparkled with perfection. One strange day, quite content that her house was shipshape, she settled into her big stuffed chair with a cup of hot chocolate when she heard something odd. It was a sneaky little sound that wasn't nice at all. In fact, it sounded very dirty! Flabbergasted at the dirty sound in her squeaky clean house, Muriel put down her hot chocolate and replaced it with her trusty mop. What a scrubbing she would give that dirty sound when she found it! She looked in the cupboard, but it wasn't there. She looked for it in the closet, but it wasn't there either. She looked and looked and looked, but she couldn't find it anywhere.

Where would we look for it?

Sometimes, even when we're trying our hardest to be good people, we miss something not-so-good about ourselves because it has hidden itself very well.

> We use this Name to help us shine the Light on that not-so-good part and bring it out of hiding!
>
> We're not saying we'll be perfect, but we will be full of Light and love!

FORGET THYSELF

להה לי

34. FORGET THYSELF

Jeffrey loved *his* ideas solely
He regarded them as holy
"Mine are best!" he said with zest
So they put them to the test
But *his* were rather less than best
They would be better put to rest!
But Jeff refused to see the truth
That his ideas were just uncouth!

Sometimes we can be our own worst enemies when we cling to our own opinions and don't open ourselves to the ideas of others.

> We use this Name to help get out of our own way and be open to new ideas.

OUR
BODIES/
OURSELVES

35. OUR BODIES/OURSELVES

Our bodies belong to us. We are their guardians.

Because we care for our bodies, we feed them healthy foods.
Because we care for our bodies, we exercise them.
Because we care for our bodies, we fill them with the Light that comes from positive actions and positive thoughts.

We must never knowingly hurt our bodies.
We must never let anyone else hurt our bodies.

This Name gives us the courage to tell someone like our parents or a teacher if someone is hurting us, or hurting our bodies.

> **We use this Name to surround ourselves in the Light's divine protection.**

FEAR (LESS)

36. FEAR(LESS)

"Being fearful stops you from getting Light, because you listen to the Opponent. You could do anything if you were fearless."
—Marcos, age 11

"Trying new challenges."
—Iris Perez, age 14

"Enjoy to not be afraid of going places alone."
—Sally, age 10

The Dark Wizard's evil power had ebbed away slowly during the last one hundred years of his reign. Having no real power left, he ruled by fear. A simple lift of an eyebrow, the lowering of his voice, and the mere mention of a spell would send would-be heroes fleeing for their lives. Oh, if only they knew that his power was a sham! But until someone stood up to him, he would rely on fear to remain in power.

One day, a small girl asked for an audience. Curious, the Dark Wizard agreed to see her. Though reed thin, she had an inner strength about her. When the Dark Wizard demanded to know what she wanted, she said mildly, "I want to see your power."

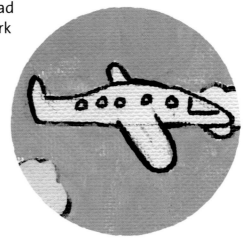

The Dark Wizard scoffed. He would not waste an ounce of his power on a meaningless girl and ordered her away.

But she would not go away, and still she insisted, "I want to see your power."

Angry, the Dark Wizard arched his eyebrow as high as it would go and deepened his voice while uttering a powerless incantation. Unlike the others who fled at the mere thought of his might, the little girl did not budge.

"I want to see your power," she said.

The Dark Wizard was enraged. How dare this speck of a girl demand anything of him?

Then he noticed her shaking knees beneath her worn and threadbare skirt. Aha! She was afraid! But no matter how much he fumed and screamed and threatened her, she did not budge. She was tired of her village living in fear of the Dark Wizard and had decided to stand up to him once and for all. If she didn't, then who would? And besides that, she had this Name . . .

Now it was the Dark Wizard who was frightened. If a wisp of a child could put her fear aside and stand up to him, then what next? A knight in shining armor with a razor-sharp sword? Throwing his cloak around him, the Dark Wizard ran for his life and was heard of no more.

The girl smiled. The Name had worked.

Sometimes our fears are greater than the real problem.

We use this Name to help face our fears and then yank them out by the roots!

THE
BIG
PICTURE

אֱ־לֹ־הַי

37. THE BIG PICTURE

Johnny loved apples. He loved to eat them whole, then spit out the seeds. One spring day, he noticed little green sprouts coming out of the ground where he had spit seeds that past winter. As time passed, he realized that the sprouts were growing into apple trees!

Now when Johnny sees an apple seed, he can't help but see the tree hidden inside of it.

Using this Name helps us see the big picture. Just as Johnny could look at a tiny seed and see the tree it would grow into one day, we can see how even our tiniest actions will grow into our future and shape who and what we are.

> **We use this Name to help us see the big picture!**

SHARING

38. SHARING

S is for **satisfied**.
H is for **holy**.
A is for **act**.
R is for **receiving**.
I is for **ignite**.
N is for **new**
G is for **goodness**.

By sharing we become **satisfied** and **holy**. By this **act**, we begin a circle of **sharing** and **receiving**. We **ignite** the light of righteousness with our new behavior and help bring **goodness** into the world.

> We use this Name to help the power of sharing make us all win!

רה״ע

DIAMOND
IN THE ROUGH
—BEING THE BEST
WE CAN BE

39. DIAMOND IN THE ROUGH—BEING THE BEST WE CAN BE

"Trying new challenges."
—Iris Perez, age 14

Recipe for making a diamond:
Take one lump of coal
Add tons of pressure
Pressurize until done and, voila!
A diamond!

Recipe for making our lives as shining as a diamond:
Take ourselves
Add the pressure of life's hardships and obstacles
Mix thoroughly with this Name and, voila!
We've transformed our problems into bright new opportunities for ourselves!

We use this Name to be the best we can be!

SPEAKING THE
RIGHT
WORDS

ל·ל·ז

40. SPEAKING THE RIGHT WORDS

Words are very, very powerful. They can be used to hurt people and they can be used to make people happy.

When we use our words to hurt people, we send darkness into the world. But when we use our words lovingly, we send only Light into the world.

The world needs our Light.

The world needs our kind words.

We use this Name to help us speak the right words!

SELF-ESTEEM

41. SELF-ESTEEM

"Lifting our self-esteem up helps lift the world."

She would rather walk up long flights of stairs than ride the elevator marked "Blacks only." She would rather go thirsty than drink from a water fountain labeled "Blacks only." She would rather be arrested—and she was!—than give up her seat on a bus to a white man. Fueled by self-esteem and determination, Rosa Parks helped spark a civil rights movement that changed the world.

We all must believe in ourselves in order to build a bridge to the Light. When we are connected, we have the power to end our problems and the problems of the world!

We use this Name to lift our self-esteem to new heights!

בוילב

FINDING THE
HIDDEN

42. FINDING THE HIDDEN

Sherlock Holmes, the fictional character created by Sir Arthur Conan Doyle, was a famous Scotland Yard detective who solved crimes by finding hidden truths.

With the help of this Name, we too can seek out the real honest-to-goodness truth!

We can be our own detectives! We can find the truth and let it out of the box!

> We use this Name to help us be our own private eyes!

DEFYING
GRAVITY

43. DEFYING GRAVITY

The sizzling lava was almost upon them. Leda yanked Neto along after her. If they didn't outrun the lava, they'd burn up just like their thatched hut did only moments ago.

Leda could go much faster if it weren't for her brother. Neto was younger than she, but he was taller and stronger. Despite this, he was ready to give up.

"I can't run anymore," he cried. "My legs hurt and we'll never make it anyway."

Leda wouldn't listen. Deep in her heart she believed escape was possible. If only Neto would believe it, too! All they had to do was jump over the gorge and they'd be safe.

"I can't make that jump," he whimpered. "Just leave me behind!"

But she wouldn't leave him behind, not for anything. Urgently, she called upon this Name and begged her brother to do the same. Still, even though his life depended on it, he was reluctant to give up all the doubt and darkness he carried inside of him.

"Do it," she cried. "Concentrate on the word!"

Thankfully, he did, and just in time they jumped! Together, they defied gravity and landed safely on the other side.

We use this Name to unleash the power of mind over matter!

יל.ד.ה

SWEETENING
JUDGMENT

44. SWEETENING JUDGMENT

Every time we say or do something bad it takes wing and flies off into the world.

Every time we say or do something good it also takes wing and flies off into the world.

When we aren't looking or expecting it, the good and the bad come flying back to us like homing pigeons.

The good ones are good for us.

The bad ones are BAD for us!

When we use this Name and are truly sorry for the bad we've said or done, we are protected. The good gets in but the bad bounces off our protective shield!

THE PATH TO
RICHES

45. THE PATH TO RICHES

This tale of King Midas is a classic myth about what happens when true happiness is given up for material riches.

King Midas possessed everything a king could want: a luxurious castle, sweet-smelling rose gardens, excellent food, and a loving daughter named Zoe. But of all the wonderful things that were his, King Midas cherished his gold above all. Daily, he would count his huge pile of gold coins then throw them up in the air and laugh giddily as they showered down around him.

One day, ~~Dionysus~~, the god ~~of celebration~~, decided to favor the king by granting him a wish. King Midas knew immediately what he would wish for.

"I wish that everything I touched turned to pure, solid, wonderful gold!"

Starting the very next morning, everything King Midas touched turned to gold. Soon he had golden chairs, golden tables, golden rugs, golden pictures, golden fireplaces, and even a golden bathtub! By the afternoon he was hungry, but when he touched his food and drink . . .

It turned to gold, too!

Fear gripped the king. What had he done? One cannot eat and drink gold! He would starve!

Hearing his cries, his daughter Zoe ran to comfort him. Though he tried to stop her, she threw her arms around him and . . .

Her warmth, her smile, and her laugh were all gone, replaced by the cold hardness of gold. Beside himself with grief, King Midas cried out to ~~Dionysus~~ to take away his golden curse.

~~Dionysus~~ could see that King Midas had learned a valuable lesson. Just to make sure, he also took away all the gold the king had ever possessed. No matter. King Midas no longer cared for gold. His happiness now came from the richness of life and the love of his daughter.

We may have lots of material riches in our lives but, like King Midas, we must never forget the true source of happiness. True happiness comes from the Light of our Creator.

> **We use this Name to invite good fortune to us through our souls and not through our greed.**

BEING
ABSOLUTELY
SURE

46. BEING ABSOLUTELY SURE

"Trust."
—April, age 13

"Exactness."
—Jasmine, age 11

"To make sure."
—Sinjin, age 13

When we are absolutely sure that we can dance, we will dance!

When we are absolutely sure that we can read, we will read!

When we are absolutely sure that we can achieve, we will achieve!

We must believe—absolutely—in our dreams.

We must believe—absolutely—in our talents and abilities.

> We use this Name to help us believe in ourselves, to help us trust in ourselves, and to help us trust in the power of the Names.

עֵשֶׂ״ל

WORLD
PEACE

47. WORLD PEACE

"How wonderful it is that nobody need wait a single moment before starting to improve the world."
—Anne Frank, a German-Jewish teenager forced into hiding during the Holocaust (1929-1945)

We cannot have peace in the world until we sow the seeds of peace in our own hearts. Once peace grows inside of us, we can help it grow throughout the world.

We use this Name to help peace grow.

מילה

UNITY

48. UNITY

The following poem is credited to John Godfrey Saxe (1816-1887). It is his version of a famous Indian legend.

The Blind Men and the Elephant

It was six men of Indostan
To learning much inclined,
Who went to see the Elephant
(Though all of them were blind),
That each by observation
Might satisfy his mind.

The First approached the Elephant,
And happening to fall
Against his broad and sturdy side,
At once began to bawl:
"God bless me! but the Elephant
Is very like a wall!"

The Second, feeling of the tusk
Cried, "Ho! What have we here,
So very round and smooth and sharp?
To me 'tis mighty clear
This wonder of an Elephant
Is very like a spear!"

The Third approached the animal,
And happening to take
The squirming trunk within his hands,
Thus boldly up he spake:
"I see," quoth he, "the Elephant
Is very like a snake!"

The Fourth reached out an eager hand,
And felt about the knee:
"What most this wondrous beast is like
Is mighty plain," quoth he;
"'Tis clear enough the Elephant
Is very like a tree!"

The Fifth, who chanced to touch the ear,
Said: "E'en the blindest man
Can tell what this resembles most;
Deny the fact who can,
This marvel of an Elephant
Is very like a fan!"

The Sixth no sooner had begun
About the beast to grope,
Than, seizing on the swinging tail
That fell within his scope.
"I see," quoth he, "the Elephant
Is very like a rope!"

And so these men of Indostan
Disputed loud and long,
Each in his own opinion
Exceeding stiff and strong,
Though each was partly in the right,
And all were in the wrong!

Like the blind men of the poem, we would often rather be right than to realize the higher truth, and that truth is unity. Unity is harmony. Unity is working together. Unity is seeing that more than one belief, idea, viewpoint, or opinion can be right. If the blind men from the poem weren't so busy arguing, perhaps they could have realized that together they "saw" the whole elephant!

We use this Name to focus on unity and harmony with our friends and family.

וִיהִיּ

HAPPINESS

49. HAPPINESS

If we listen to what commercials tell us, then . . .

Using the right toothpaste will make us happy.

New toys will make us happy.

Expensive clothes will make us happy.

French fries, hamburgers, and soda will make us happy.

And maybe they do . . . for a little while.

For a lasting happiness that will stay with us long after we've eaten our French fries, or after the pants we wanted so badly have gone out of style, we use this Name.

> We use this Name to find true happiness because true happiness feeds our souls!

ד.ג.י

ENOUGH IS NEVER ENOUGH

"Life begets life. Energy becomes energy. It is by spending oneself that one becomes rich."
—Sarah Bernhardt, actress (1844-1923)

50. ENOUGH IS NEVER ENOUGH

Taylor loved to stretch his hands up to the moon. "Moooon!" he would say in his baby voice. "Me want to touch the moon, Zellie!"

His big sister, Zelda, would always say, "Enough with that, Taylor! You'll never touch the moon."

When Taylor got older, he studied science very hard. Still his sister would say, "Enough with that, Taylor! You'll never go to college."

As the years slipped away, any dreams Zelda had slipped away, too, and she settled into a life that gave her just enough to live but not much more.

Meanwhile, Taylor's hopes and dreams urged him on. He worked hard and got a scholarship to college. After that, he became an astronaut.

One day, he put a strange-looking rock on Zelda's kitchen table. As she dried her hands from doing dishes, she asked him what it was.

"It's a moon rock," he said, his eyes gleaming.

Zelda was shocked, then tears filled her eyes. She had let her dreams go but her little brother hadn't. Just enough wasn't enough for him. Taylor had touched the moon.

God wants us not to think small.

God wants us to have it all!

> **We use this Name to never ever settle for less than the Light wants us to have!**

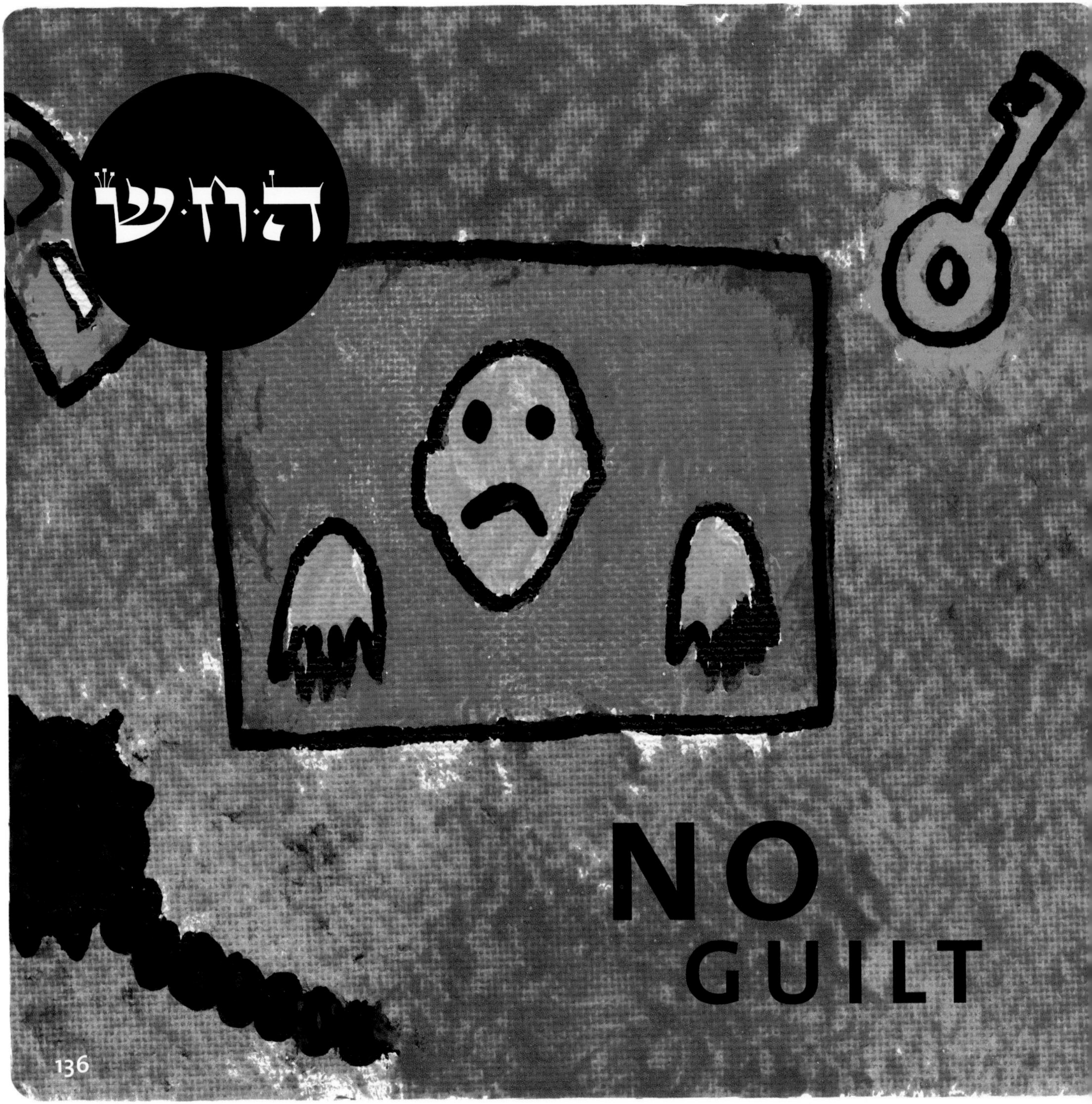
ה·ח·ט
NO
GUILT

51. NO GUILT

"Express your inner feelings! Happy that my guilt is gone."
—*Sinjin, age 13*

Adam's hand still hurt from hitting the smaller boy, but the pain was bigger than just his hand. Adam felt the pain of guilt. He wanted to apologize to the smaller boy for the injury he had caused, but how? Every time the smaller boy saw him, he took off running. Everyone at school was calling Adam a bully and now he had no friends. What could he do to take back all the hurt he had caused?

We use this Name to travel back in time to the exact moment when we did something hurtful. The hurt we caused is then erased, but only if we are truly sorry and are willing to change ourselves.

GUILT -BE- GONE

ELIMINATES GUILT ON CONTACT!

PASSION

52. PASSION

Many years ago, a boy who could not speak attended worship services with his father and mother. The boy was moved by the prayers of the others and yearned to join them, but his mouth and tongue could not form any words. Finally, his yearning became so great that he pulled out his whistle and blew it as hard as he could. Everyone gasped! How dare this boy blow a whistle in their house of prayer! But their wise worship leader could see the fire in the boy's heart; he could feel his passion to connect to the Light. He praised the boy and told everyone to delight in his whistle because its pure sound had carried their prayers directly to heaven.

We use this Name to light the fire of passion in our souls.

NO
AGENDA

53. NO AGENDA

Some of us have become someone's friend because they have better toys than us, or are richer than us . . .

Some of us feel our friends owe us something because we did something for them . . .

Some of us give a gift and expect to get one back . . .

Some of us do good deeds and expect a reward . . .

This Name helps us erase any secret plots or plans we may have when it comes to friends or acts of giving.

> When we use this Name, it clears the way for friendships and experiences based on love, joy, and true giving and sharing.

נ.ל.ת

THE DEATH OF DEATH

54. THE DEATH OF DEATH

There once was a king ruled over a wondrous land that had never known hunger or pain. One day, the angel of death passed over the land and found it so appealing that he moved in. Soon animals and crops were dying, businesses were failing, and marriages and old friendships were falling apart. The death of all things good now hung over every corner of the land. The king was so saddened by his people's suffering that he could not eat or drink.

Then a wise man came to the land and taught the king this Name.

The king mustered every ounce of his remaining strength to focus on the Name. The Name burned so brightly in his heart that finally the angel of death packed up and moved away. But by then, the king was so weak he was in danger of dying.

Gasping for breath, the king used the last of his strength to teach the Name to the people. The Name burned brightly in their hearts and with it they chased out every last speck of death the angel had left behind. In a short time, the king recovered and lived to rule for many, many years.

Death doesn't only mean that somebody dies. It can also mean the end of a friendship or family, a way of life, or the failure of a business.

We use this Name to chase away the angel of death once and for all!

THOUGHT
INTO
ACTION

בס״ד

144

55. THOUGHT INTO ACTION

"Believing in yourself."
—Soledad Fajardo, age 12

"I have a dream that one day . . . little black boys and black girls will be able to join hands with little white boys and white girls as sisters and brothers. I have a dream today."
—Martin Luther King, Jr., civil rights leader (1929-1968)

Thanks to the hard work of many, Martin Luther King's dream of true equality for all—no matter the color of their skin, their sex, their religion, or their social standing—is beginning to come true. Dreams can come true, but only if we are willing to act upon them.

We must be willing to do the work.

We must not wait.

We must not give up.

Many of us have wonderful ideas that we can't make happen because we've lost our connection to the Light.

> **We use this Name to plug into the Light and turn on our ideas!**

פ·ר·י

GETTING
RID OF
ANGER

56. GETTING RID OF ANGER

"Calming down first then reacting and saying a bad thing to someone."
—Maribel Ramos, age 13

"Get rid of all hatred and madness in your body."
—Darren Valenzuela, age 9

"I will permit no man to narrow and degrade my soul by making me hate him."
—Booker T. Washington, African-American educator and leader (1856-1915)

"Holding on to anger is like grasping a hot coal with the intent of throwing it at someone else; you are the one who gets burned."
—Buddha, Indian philosopher and founder of Buddhism (B.C. 560-480)

"Men in rage strike those that wish them best."
—William Shakespeare, English writer and poet (1564-1616)

"If you are patient in one moment of anger, you will escape a hundred days of sorrow."
—Chinese proverb

We use this Name to become anger free!

נ.מ.ם

LISTENING TO
OUR SOUL
—THE GOOD GUY

57. LISTENING TO OUR SOUL —THE GOOD GUY

Do you listen to your soul

To the beat of rock 'n' roll?

Or as wind whispering through trees?

Perhaps you do on bended knee.

Use this Name!

The soul's mission is found!

From inside you comes its gentle sound.

> When we use this Name, the whispers of our souls and the true yearnings of our hearts are heard. If we listen carefully, our souls will lead us to where we need to be.

LETTING
GO

58. LETTING GO

Malcolm was depressed. When he was little, he and his family lived in a dumpy apartment. When he was little, they barely had enough to eat. When he was little, there was no Christmas or birthdays or any holidays because his mother never had any money. But after she remarried they had lots of money. His mom had another baby, a girl, who had no idea of what growing up without food or toys or decent clothes was like.

"It's not fair!" Malcolm screamed at his mom. "She has it so good and I had it so bad!"

"But things are different now, Malcolm," his mom said, rubbing his shoulder. "Can't you enjoy how good it is now?"

Malcolm wanted to. He wanted to finally enjoy his life, but he was scared. What if it was all too good to be true? What if it all went away someday?

"You've got to let go of the past," his mother said gently. "You've got to let it go."

If we hold onto an ugly past, we can't have a beautiful future.

> **We use this Name and "let go!"**

FEELING
SAFE

59. FEELING SAFE

"Secure angels are with you, Light helping you out."
—Jazmin Sanchez, age 11

Question: How many kids who use this Name does it take to screw in a light bulb?

Answer: None! They don't need a light bulb! They carry their Light within them!

We use this Name to plug into the Light. When the going gets rough, plug in!

מוּצָר

FREEDOM

154

60. FREEDOM

"Have the freedom to live in the USA and the right to be here and the right to believe in yourself."
—Celine, age 13

The children of Israel had been enslaved in Egypt for four hundred years when Moses came and led them to freedom. However, before they reached the freedom of the Promised Land, the Israelites faced a hard journey. They braved crossing the Red Sea with the army of Pharaoh right behind them, and then wandered the desert for forty years!

Even before the Israelites entered the desert, they complained about its hardships. This Moses didn't understand. How could the desert be worse than four hundred years of slavery?

The story of Moses is really a secret code. The story is really about our spiritual path. Seeking the Light is hard at times. We often want to go back and be what we were before—even if what we were wasn't very good! Why do we do that? Perhaps because it's easier to stay the same than it is to change ourselves.

When we use this Name, we have the strength to take our journey. We break the chains holding us back and journey like the Israelites to freedom.

> **We use this Name to gain our freedom.**

WATER

61. WATER

"A clear view of your life, a fountain of love."
—Diana Matamoros, age 13

The Teachings of the Rain God (adapted from a story by the Masai tribe of Kenya).

One day, the elephant said to the Rain God:

"What would happen if I tore off all the grass, all the trees, and all the bushes from the earth?"

"Doing that would not be wise, for you would have nothing to eat," answered the Rain God.

The elephant didn't believe the Rain God, so he tore off all the trees, the bushes, and the grass with his trunk and destroyed all the green of the earth.

This made the Rain God so angry that he stopped sending rain. Soon, deserts covered the earth and the elephant was dying of thirst.

The elephant said, "Rain God, I misbehaved! I was arrogant and foolish. Please forgive me and let the rain come!"

The Rain God pitied the foolish elephant, so he sent just enough rain to form a tiny pool in front of where the elephant lived. The elephant was so happy to have water, but he would not share a drop of it. One by one, all the animals of the world came and asked for a drink, but he turned them away!

Finally the lion came and asked for a drink. The elephant told him to go away, but the lion drank anyway. The elephant raised his foot and was about to stomp on the lion when the Rain God sent down a bolt of lighting and said:

"Water is my gift to all creatures, elephant! Water is life! You must learn to protect what you will all need in the future!"

From this the elephant learned to share what he had. He also learned that water is divine and feeds the whole world.

Pure, clean water has power. Water quenches our thirst, grows our food, cleans us, and heals us. But just as we've polluted our rivers, oceans, and lakes, we've also polluted the water that makes up 65 percent of our bodies.

> We use this Name to clean the waters of earth and the water of our bodies to be strong and healthy!

TEACHER, NOT PREACHER

62. TEACHER, NOT PREACHER

Most of us don't like to be told what to do, even if it's for our own good! If people are always telling us, "Do this! Do that!" we think they're bossy.

Are we ever bossy?

Are we always telling our little brother or sister or our friends what to do?

This Name helps us live in the truth. Our good words and deeds help light the way for our friends and family to follow. And they follow because they want to, not because we're pushing them!

> **We use this Name to become a teacher, not a preacher.**

עב־נ־ו

APPRECIATION

63. APPRECIATION

There once was a man named Sam who had a very small house. It was very nice, mind you, but it was just so small that he and his wife and his five children were very cramped inside it. Longing to have a bigger house, Sam asked the village wise man what to do. And the wise man said:

"Move your cow into the house."

Sam could not believe his ears! Move his cow into the house? But since the wise man was very wise, Sam moved his cow into the house. Now they were even more cramped than before, so Sam went back to the wise man and told him how things had gone from bad to worse. And the wise man said:

"Move your horse into the house."

Again, Sam could not believe his ears. His horse? But since the wise man was very wise, Sam moved his horse into the house. Now it was so crowded that they all had to stand shoulder to shoulder. Desperate, Sam went back to see the wise man. And the wise man said:

"Move your chickens into the house."

Reluctantly, Sam did as he was told and moved all twenty-eight of his chickens into the house. Now they were so very crowded that they had to stand on each other's shoulders!

Unable to bear this condition a moment longer, Sam went back to the wise man and begged for help. He must have a bigger house! This time, the wise man said:

"Move all of the animals out of your house."

And Sam did. Now he couldn't believe how big his house was! It was a miracle!

Do some of us find that we only appreciate things after they're gone?

Maybe we forget to brush our teeth sometimes but then a toothache helps remind us how nice it is to have healthy teeth.

Maybe we fight with our sister but after she's away at college we remember how nice it was to have her around.

We use this Name to appreciate all the wonderful things we DO have right now!

מוזי

BELIEVING IN OURSELVES
—PUTTING OURSELVES IN A GOOD LIGHT

64. BELIEVING IN OURSELVES—PUTTING OURSELVES IN A GOOD LIGHT

When we focus on all the bad stuff about ourselves, other people do, too. For example:

"Look at this horrible pimple on my face! It makes me look awful!"

"Now that you've pointed it out to me (because I didn't notice it before), yes, it does make you look awful."

"It does? Aaaaaaa!"

But if we give people good reasons to focus on the good stuff about us, a warm Light surrounds us and protects us from the bad thoughts of others.

> We use this Name to help others see all the good stuff in us!

THE LIGHT

"A good thing that can help you; something that makes you happy, makes you share and not listen to bad things."
—Celene, age 13

65. THE LIGHT

The last real thing Alicia remembered was a giant flat saucer-like thing hovering over her. It was like something you'd see in a movie about aliens. That's it! It was a spaceship! Then she remembered floating up toward it. And now, here she was back in her backyard like nothing had happened. Even the sprinklers she was running through before the saucer thingy came were still on. But something must have happened because everything seemed slightly different to her. The trees looked like trees, yet they seemed more alive than ever. She could even see a faint light shimmering inside of them.

Then Alicia's brother, Alex, slammed out of the back door.

"Alicia! Can I borrow your bike? I know you never let me, but *please*?"

Alicia looked at her brother. He looked like he always had, but different, too. For the first time, she noticed how his hair fell around his soft blue eyes and how he tended to stand kind of crooked, putting more weight on his right foot than on his left. More important, she noticed a faint light glowing inside of him. It was just like the light inside of the tree. In fact, it was just like the light she was now seeing in everything around her! Somehow, everything seemed clear and bright, and all Alicia could feel was love. Normally, she wouldn't let her brother borrow anything of hers, but now she felt like sharing.

Though the story about Alicia is just made up, it has a meaning to it: We don't have to go up in a spaceship to change the way we see the world and the people in it. All we need is the Light.

> We use this Name to see the Light of our Creator in every person. We will become wiser. We will see that sharing helps us and helps the world.

מֶנְק

RESPONSIBLE
FOR YOUR
ACTIONS

66. RESPONSIBLE FOR YOUR ACTIONS

"It's your fault. Look at your own self."
—Malik, age 8

Have you ever said something like, "Why does everything bad happen to me? I didn't do anything!"

Sometimes it seems as though life can be hurtful. This gives us two choices:
1. We can hold on to the pain and feel sorry for ourselves.
2. We can use the experience to rise above our problems.

Any wrong done to us is because somewhere in our lives we did something wrong to someone else.

We use this Name to give up feeling sorry for ourselves.

We use this Name to understand that "getting back" at someone hurts us as well as them.

We use this Name to become the masters of our own bright future by making good choices and also taking responsibility for the not-so-good choices as well.

א·י·ע

GREAT
EXPECTATIONS
—WANTING THE BEST

67. GREAT EXPECTATIONS—WANTING THE BEST

Shanti had been the queen's servant ever since she was sold into slavery at age seven. Now, at thirteen, she longed for her freedom. Shanti decided to work very hard and, in that way, gain the queen's favor. It was common knowledge that if the queen favored a slave, she would set her free.

Shanti's effort seemed to be working, too, because the queen often commented on her good work.

Days turned into weeks and weeks to months, and Shanti continued to work hard. But nothing was changing. The queen hadn't favored her at all and she was still a slave. So Shanti gave up.

Now Shanti was really miserable. In giving up, she also gave up working to the best of her ability, and now she missed the pleasure she received from doing a job well.

So Shanti began to work hard again—not for the queen or for any reward she might receive, but for herself. Days and weeks and months went by, but this time Shanti barely noticed them passing.

And then, when she least expected it, the queen gave Shanti her freedom.

This Name helps us gain control over time.

We use this Name to help us be grateful for what we have in this moment.

CONTACTING
DEPARTED SOULS

68. CONTACTING DEPARTED SOULS

"To live is to go on a journey; to die is to come back home."
—Author Unknown

"The spirit world is not far away. Sometimes the veil between this life and the life beyond becomes very thin. Our loved ones who have passed on are not far from us."
—Ezra Taft Benson, thirteenth president of The Church of Jesus Christ of Latter-day Saints (1899-1994)

> With this Name we remind ourselves of our loved ones who are no longer with us. We surround them with Light. We open ourselves to their wisdom and guidance.

LOST AND FOUND

רא.ה

69. LOST AND FOUND

Jake was lost and oh so alone
Which was the way to find his home?
Learned him this Name . . .
It saved the day!
Confused no more, Jake found his way.

There are times when we all find ourselves lost and confused. We may become lost while trying to get somewhere or we may become confused trying to find our way through life.

We use this Name to help us find the right path home.

ל-ב-נ

SEEING THE
BIGGER PLAN
WHEN EVERYTHING
LOOKS WRONG

70. SEEING THE BIGGER PLAN WHEN EVERYTHING LOOKS WRONG

The Crow and the Pitcher (adapted from an Aesop fable)

After a long flight, a crow was dying of thirst. He had taken this long trip many times and there was always plenty of water around, but today there was none to be found. Panic gripped the crow. He wanted to cry out for help but his throat was too dry. His head was spinning with fear. He was going to die!

Then he saw a water jug not far off. When he flew to it, he found only a little water inside and, worse yet, his beak couldn't reach through the jug's narrow opening. Even with water so close, he was going to perish!

Then, a voice deep within him said to accept this hardship and quiet himself, and so he did. Suddenly, the pebbles surrounding the water jug grabbed his attention and an idea took hold.

He collected the pebbles with his beak and one by one dropped them into the jug until the water was within his reach. Now he could drink easily.

His clear thinking had saved his life.

We all face problems that scare us, but if we accept hardship as a chance to grow, we move closer to the Light.

> We use this Name when we find ourselves full of doom and gloom. We use this Name to help us understand that all things happen for a reason.

הׁ·ׁי·ׁי

PROPHECY
AND
DIFFERENT WORLDS

71. PROPHECY AND DIFFERENT WORLDS

Prophecy is being able to see our own future based on what we are choosing to do now.

If we choose to steal . . .

If we choose to lie . . .

If we choose to fight needlessly . . .

If we choose to be selfish . . .

Then we choose to live in a world filled with our own unhappiness. We have created that unhappy world with our actions.

But if we choose to live lives of sharing . . .

Caring . . .

Forgiveness . . .

Love . . .

Then we choose to live in a world filled with happiness and joy. We have created that world with our actions.

Our actions create our futures; they create the world we choose to live in.

> **We use this Name to help us enter a world full of Light.**

מ·ו·ם

SPIRITUAL CLEANSING
—BECOMING A BETTER PERSON

"Sharing candy, sharing Light, too."
—*Ernesto Argota, age 12*

Deborah was always sick. If it wasn't a toothache, it was a bellyache. If it wasn't a bad boyfriend, it was just a bad friend in general. Nothing ever seemed to go right in her life and she was tired of all the pain.

Then one night she had a strange dream.

In it, she saw different kinds of people who lived in different time periods. She saw different men and different women who had different skin colors, different languages, and lived in countries she'd never been to, at least not in her present life.

But there was one thing that these people had in common. In her dream, Deborah could see that none of them were very nice. All of them made choices that made others suffer.

The next morning when Deborah awoke, she realized something big. Her dream was telling her something. It was telling her that she, Deborah Lee Jordan, had once been all of those people who weren't very nice!

Now Deborah knew that if she wanted to stop her own suffering she must clean up her past, including her past lives! So here's what she did:

she used this Name to cleanse her soul. It was like taking a nice hot shower. When she was done, she felt squeaky clean! But Deborah was not going to stop there. From now on, she would live a life of caring and sharing. She would keep her soul sparkling clean!

When we use this Name we push REWIND and erase all the bad stuff we did in past lives.

We use this Name and get a brand-new beginning!

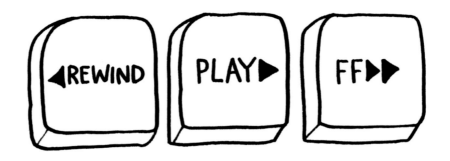

LIST OF 72 NAMES (TRANSLITERATIONS)

1.	וָהֶו	VAV HEY VAV	(Time Travel)
2.	יְלִי	YUD LAMED YUD	(Recapturing the Sparks)
3.	סִיט	SAMECH YUD TET	(Miracle Making)
4.	עָלַם	AYIN LAMED MEM	(Getting Rid of Negative Thoughts)
5.	מַהְשׁ	MEM HEY SHIN	(Healing)
6.	לָלָה	LAMED LAMED HEY	(Dream State)
7.	אָכָא	ALEPH KAF ALEPH	(Connecting to Our Soul)
8.	כַּהַת	KAF HEY TAV	(Sending Away Negative Energy)
9.	הָזִי	HEY ZAYIN YUD	(Angelic Powers)
10.	אֶלָד	ALEPH LAMED DALED	(Protection from the Evil Eye)
11.	לָאו	LAMED ALEPH VAV	(Throwing Away Evil's Leftovers)
12.	הַהַע	HEY HEY AYIN	(Unconditional Love)
13.	יֵזַל	YUD ZAYIN LAMED	(Heaven on Earth)
14.	מֵבַה	MEM BET HEY	(Stop the Fighting)
15.	הָרִי	HEY RESH YUD	(Long-Range Vision—Eye That Can See for a Mile!)
16.	הָקֶם	HEY KUF MEM	(Giving the Boot to Sadness)
17.	לָאו	LAMED ALEPH VAV	(Great Escape)
18.	כְּלִי	KAF LAMED YUD	(Fertility)
19.	לָוו	LAMED VAV VAV	(Dialing God)
20.	פָּהֵל	PEY HEY LAMED	(Winning Big over Bad Habits)
21.	נָלָך	NUN LAMED KAF	(No More Sickness)
22.	ייי	YUD YUD YUD	(Stopping the Wrong People from Coming into Our Lives)
23.	מֵלָה	MEM LAMED HEY	(Sharing the Flame)
24.	וָחַו	CHET HEY VAV	(Jealousy)

25.	נתה	NUN TAV HEY	(Speaking Our Minds)
26.	האא	HEY ALEPH ALEPH	(How to Straighten up a Big Mess)
27.	ירת	YUD RESH TAV	(Silent Partner)
28.	שאה	SHIN ALEPH HEY	(Soul Mate)
29.	ריי	RESH YUD YUD	(Getting Rid of Hate)
30.	אום	ALEPH VAV MEM	(Building Bridges)
31.	לכב	LAMED KAF BET	(Finishing What We Start)
32.	ושר	VAV SHIN RESH	(Memories)
33.	יחו	YUD CHET VAV	(Revealing the Dark Side)
34.	להח	LAMED HEY CHET	(Forget Thyself)
35.	כוק	KAF VAV KUF	(Sexual Energy)
36.	מנד	MEM NUN DALED	(Fear(less))
37.	אני	ALEPH NUN YUD	(The Big Picture)
38.	חעם	CHET AYIN MEM	(Sharing)
39.	רהע	RESH HEY AYIN	(Diamond in the Rough—Being the Best We Can Be)
40.	ייז	YUD YUD ZAYIN	(Speaking the Right Words)
41.	ההה	HEY HEY HEY	(Self-Esteem)
42.	מיכ	MEM YUD KAF	(Finding the Hidden)
43.	וול	VAV VAV LAMED	(Defying Gravity)
44.	ילה	YUD LAMED HEY	(Sweetening Judgement)
45.	סאל	SAMECH ALEPH LAMED	(The Path to Riches)
46.	ערי	AYIN RESH YUD	(Being Absolutely Sure)
47.	עשל	AYIN SHIN LAMED	(World Peace)
48.	מיה	MEM YUD HEY	(Unity)

49.	וְהוּ	VAV HEY VAV	(Happiness)
50	דְּנִי	DALED NUN YUD	(Enough Is Never Enough)
51	הֲחֶשׁ	HEY CHET SHIN	(No Guilt)
52	עֲמָם	AYIN MEM MEM	(Passion)
53	נְנָא	NUN NUN ALEPH	(No Agenda)
54	נִית	NUN YUD TAV	(The Death of Death)
55	מְבַה	MEM BET HEY	(Thought into Action)
56	פֻּוִי	PEY VAV YUD	(Getting Rid of Anger)
57	נְמָם	NUN MEM MEM	(Listening to Our Soul—The Good Guy)
58	יֵיל	YUD YUD LAMED	(Letting Go)
59	הֲרֻו	HEY RESH CHET	(Feeling Safe)
60	מְצֶר	MEM ZADIK RESH	(Freedom)
61	וּמָב	VAV MEM BET	(Water)
62	יְהַה	YUD HEY HEY	(Teacher, Not Preacher)
63	עֲנוּ	AYIN NUN VAV	(Appreciation)
64	מְחִי	MEM CHET YUD	(Believing in Ourselves—Putting Ourselves in a Good Light)
65	דְּמָב	DALED MEM BET	(The Light)
66	מְנָק	MEM NUN KUF	(Responsible for Your Actions)
67	אֵיעַ	ALEPH YUD AYIN	(Great Expectations—Wanting the Best)
68	וְהֻו	CHET BET VAV	(Contacting Departed Souls)
69	רֶאַה	RESH ALEPH HEY	(Lost and Found)
70	יְבֵם	YUD BET MEM	(Seeing the Bigger Plan When Everything Looks Wrong)
71	הֲיִי	HEY YUD YUD	(Prophecy and Different Worlds)
72	מֻום	MEM VAV MEM	(Spiritual Cleansing—Becoming a Better Person)

MAY WE ALL FIND THE JOY AND HAPPINESS THE LIGHT WANTS US TO HAVE!

The knowledge of the 72 Names of God comes from the teachings of Kabbalah. Kabbalah is over 4,000 years old. It began with Abraham, who was the father of the three great religions: Judaism, Christianity, and Islam. Abraham discovered a code of laws for how the universe works. This code explained how the physical world (what we can see, touch, hear, taste, and smell) meets with the spiritual world (what we can't see, hear, taste, touch, or smell).

To learn more about Kabbalah and the 72 Names of God, you and your parents can call 1-800-KABBALAH or visit our Web site at www.72.com.

I wish that The 72 Names of God will enlighten and empower
my kids Jonathan Natasha-Deborah and Joseph—together
with all the children of the world—to make the right choice
and the light choice in every aspect of their lives.

I wish for the quick and complete recovery of Rav Berg,
to whom I am forever indebted.

I wish that I, my mom, my brother and sisters and all the adults
of the world will participate in and witness a world without
chaos, suffering, or hatred.

I wish for a world filled with miracles and wonders, and may
death disappear forever.

Isaac ben Mordechay Novian

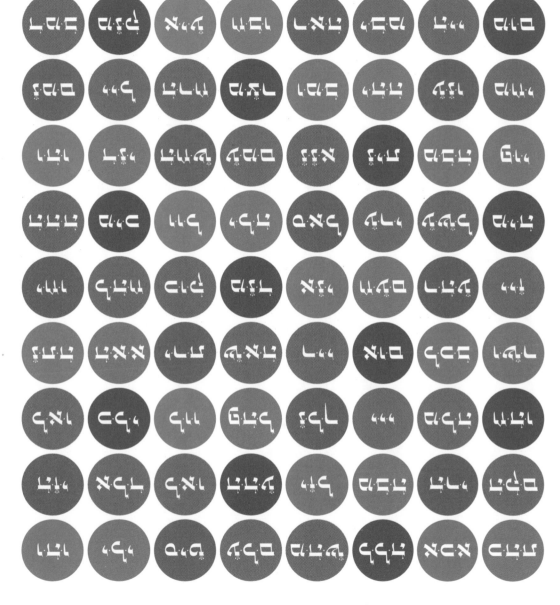